NEW VANGUARD 327

GERMAN TANKS IN FRANCE 1940

Armor in the Wehrmacht's greatest
Blitzkrieg victory

STEVEN J. ZALOGA · ILLUSTRATED BY FELIPE RODRÍGUEZ

OSPREY PUBLISHING

Bloomsbury Publishing Plc

Kemp House, Chawley Park, Cumnor Hill, Oxford OX2 9PH, UK

29 Earlsfort Terrace, Dublin 2, Ireland

1385 Broadway, 5th Floor, New York, NY 10018, USA

E-mail: info@ospreypublishing.com

www.ospreypublishing.com

OSPREY is a trademark of Osprey Publishing Ltd

First published in Great Britain in 2024

A catalog record for this book is available from the British Library.

ISBN: PB 9781472859440; eBook 9781472859457;
ePDF 9781472859471; XML: 9781472859464

24 25 26 27 28 10 9 8 7 6 5 4 3 2 1

Index by Fionbar Lyons

Typeset by PDQ Digital Media Solutions, Bungay, UK
Printed and bound in India by Replika Press Private Ltd.

Title page image: see p. 12

AUTHOR'S NOTE

The Wehrmacht in World War II often listed tank gun calibers in centimeters, but in this book they are shown in the more familiar millimeters for consistency. All photos in this book are from the US National Archives and Records Administration II in College Park, Maryland.

Glossary

A.K.	*Armee-Korps* (Army Corps)
DCr	*Division cuirasée* (French armored division)
DLM	*Division légère mécanique* (French mechanized cavalry division)
Gen d.Art	*General der Artillerie*
Gen d.Kav	*General der Kavallerie*
GenObst	*General Oberst* (Colonel-General)
Gen d.Pz	*General der Panzerwaffe*
KwK	*Kampfwagen Kanone* (Tank Gun)
SR	*Schützen Regiment* (Rifle Regiment)
RTR	Royal Tank Regiment
PaK	*Panzerabwehrkanone* (Anti-tank gun)
PzKpfw	*Panzerkampfwagen* (Tank)
(t)	*Tschechisch* (Czech, e.g. PzKpfw 38(t))

CONTENTS

GERMAN TANKS IN FRANCE 1940

Armor in the Wehrmacht's greatest Blitzkrieg victory

INTRODUCTION

The rapid defeat of France in 1940 was a military catastrophe. In contrast to the prolonged and bloody battles of 1914–1918, new mechanized operations provided novel means to conduct a rapid and decisive encirclement battle in less than a month. Panzers were at the heart of these new tactics. Sometimes called *Blitzkrieg*, in recent years this term has been challenged by historians as a journalistic invention rather than an actual concept. Regardless of the terminology, the Battle of France demonstrated the combat effectiveness of combined-arms mechanized operations.

DOCTRINE AND ORGANIZATION

Germany's tank force during World War I was miniscule, consisting mainly of war-booty tanks and a handful of locally produced A7Vs. German interest in Panzers changed dramatically after the war. The Versailles Treaty ending World War I forbade Germany from creating a new tank force. Paradoxically, the ban on German tanks made them all-the-more alluring for the German Army. The usual resistance from conservative officers seen in other European armies was far less potent in Germany, a perverse consequence of the Versailles Treaty.

The two most common tank types in the 7.Panzer Division in 1940 were the PzKpfw II Ausf. C (left) and the PzKpfw 38(t) (foreground).

The genesis of the Panzer divisions can be traced back to early efforts to motorize German infantry. By the late 1920s, the *Reichswehr* had begun the clandestine formation of experimental mechanized units. The promotion of a future Panzer force was sponsored by the *Inspektor für Heeresmotorisierung* (Inspector for Motorized Troops) headed after 1931 by Genmaj Oswald Lutz and his chief of staff, ObstLt Heinz Guderian. Lutz was the architect of the early Panzer force; Guderian was its most vocal proponent.

Rather than viewing tanks as some radical break from tradition, the proponents of the Panzerwaffe depicted them as a futuristic extension to the lessons learnt in World War I. Specialized storm troops had used infiltration tactics to overcome the static warfare of 1914–1918, and this served as a template for Panzer tactics. Panzer divisions could transform infiltration tactics to the operational level, returning decisive mobility to the modern battlefield. The early promotion of the Panzerwaffe by proponents in the Reichswehr was reinforced by Hitler's rise to power. Hitler's political radicalism included an enthusiasm for military futurism that enthusiastically supported the army's visionary thinkers. On seeing an early demonstration of PzKpfw I tanks, Hitler blurted out "That's what I want!" This provided the fiscal resources and government support needed to field the first large Panzer formations.

The first Panzer unit was clandestinely formed at Zossen in November 1933 as an experimental training unit. An initial plan for an experimental Panzer division was distributed within the army in October 1934. In January 1935, Lutz outlined the formation of the first three Panzer divisions and three Panzer brigades. Hitler supported the motorization of the cavalry, and so the proposed Panzer brigades were converted from horse cavalry regiments. An alternative scheme was promoted by the general staff to create enough Panzer regiments to support each of the infantry divisions. This plan was unrealistic in view of the large number of tanks required. Instead, the general staff proposed to create a Panzer regiment for each of the 12 army corps.

With 300 PzKpfw I in service in the summer of 1935, the first Panzer division was organized near Münster. Four more followed through 1939 as more tanks became available. The Panzer divisions were envisioned

Rommel's *Gefechtsstaffel* in action with a mixed formation of PzKpfw II and PzKpfw 38(t). Rommel created an informal "action squadron" to accompany him, based on radio and command tanks of the Panzer Brigade.11 headquarters company. On the horizon are a few PzKpfw IVs used to shield the Gefechtsstaffel, while in the foreground to the lower right is a Panzerbefehlswagen 38(t) with its distinctive radio mast over the rear engine deck.

A 4.7cm Panzerjäger I of Pz.Jg. Abt.643 with the 12.Armee in Heeregruppe A, passing through a town with a World War I British tank memorial in the background. This battalion named their vehicles after towns, in this case, Aschaffenburg.

as combined-arms formations, including tank, infantry, artillery, and engineer components. The early Panzer divisions had their infantry and armor sections under separate headquarters, a Schützen Brigade and a Panzer Brigade. Regardless of official tables of organization and equipment, shortages of both tanks and trained troops meant that Panzer division organization in 1938–1940 was in constant flux. Some Panzer divisions had two infantry regiments, while others had only one. The core of each of the Panzer divisions was the armored component, which usually included two Panzer regiments.

At first, the Panzer regiments were equipped with the PzKpfw I and PzKpfw II light tanks. The usual organization of the regiment's two battalions was to mix the PzKpfw I and PzKpfw II in three of the companies and to equip the fourth company entirely with PzKpfw IIs. The mixture of multiple types in a single company was criticized after the Polish campaign as a logistical headache. However, it would have been dangerous to concentrate all the PzKpfw Is in a single company due to their shortcomings, so a mixed light tank company remained standard in 1940.

As the new PzKpfw III and PzKpfw IV became available, they were generally consolidated into a medium tank company in each battalion. So, by the time of the Battle of France, the Panzer battalions consisted of four tank companies: HQ company (*Stabskompanie*), a medium tank company and two light tank companies. The headquarters companies were equipped with two small command tanks (*kleiner Panzerbefehlswagen*) based on the

A **PZKPFW I IN THE BATTLE OF FRANCE**

1. PzKpfw I Ausf. B, Aufklarungs Zug, Stab, 2./Pz.Rgt.36, 4.Panzer Division, Belgium 1940

This PzKpfw I Ausf. B carries the typical markings for a reconnaissance platoon of the headquarters company. The "L" in the tactical number indicates that the 2.Abteilung was a light battalion. On the rear plate is the divisional insignia, a yellow crow's foot in a circle. The standard Wehrmacht air identification marking in 1940 was a rectangle roughly 50 × 80cm. Black and white photos show this as white, but British army 1940 intelligence reports indicated that examples were found in yellow and orange. Some black and white film of the era registers yellow as white, so it is possible that this marking was in fact yellow. In this example, the rectangle is oriented longitudinally, but it was more often seen latitudinally across the engine deck.

2. PzKpfw I Ausf. B, 6.Kompanie, Pz.Rgt.1, 1.Panzer Division, Belgium 1940

The 1.Panzer Division had two alternative divisional markings in 1940, a single yellow dot as seen to the left of the tactical number on the turret and a white oak leaf as seen on the turret rear. The turret tactical number indicates 6.Kompanie, 2.Zug (platoon), Panzer Nr. 3. The standard camouflage scheme on Wehrmacht tanks in 1938–40 was an overall finish of Dunkelgrau Nr. 46 (dark gray), later redesignated as RAL 7021. A secondary pattern of Nr. 45 Dunkelbraun (dark brown), later RAL 7017, was airbrushed in irregular patches covering about a third of the surface. This pattern is nearly impossible to detect on black and white photos of the period, since both colors were so similar in tone. On July 1, 1940, the OKH (Army High Command) issued instructions to drop the secondary dark brown in favor of overall dark gray to conserve paint. However, tanks already painted in the two-color scheme were not immediately affected.

1

2

PzKpfw I chassis, as well as five or six light tanks for security and liaison. The regimental and battalion commanders were allotted one of the new Befehlspanzer III, a command tank version of the PzKpfw III.

However, combined-arms tactics were still in their infancy. The infantry in the Panzer divisions was motorized, but not yet mechanized. The standard means for transporting the infantry was the Krupp L2H143 truck, which could carry eight riflemen in addition to the driver. So each infantry section (*Zug*) required two trucks. These early infantry vehicles had marginal cross-country capability and were road-bound in many circumstances. The trucks served as a mode of transportation, but the riflemen dismounted from the vehicles before reaching the battlefield and fought on foot. This created a tactical dilemma regarding the coordination of Panzer and infantry troops. If the Panzers waited for the accompanying infantry, the pace of the advance would inevitably be slowed down. As a result, the Panzer divisions tended to fight with separate brigades, the Panzer brigades and the Schützen brigades performing their missions autonomously.

The technical solution to this tactical dilemma was to develop an infantry vehicle better able to keep up with the tanks in cross-country maneuver. This would permit more refined combined-arms tactics and permit battlefield integration below regimental level. Such a vehicle, the Sd.Kfz.251 infantry half-track, started to enter production in 1939. At the time of the Battle of France in 1940, there were less than a dozen companies of these armored half-tracks, and so they were not yet available in sufficient numbers to upgrade the combined-arms tactics.

Cavalry mechanization took place in parallel with the conversion of horse cavalry units into the new *leichte Division* (Light Division). This formation was intended for traditional cavalry roles such as reconnaissance and exploitation, but it lacked the full offensive power of the Panzer division. These divisions had a smaller tank complement, usually a single tank battalion, three or four *Kavallerie Schützen* (motorized dragoon) battalions, a motorcycle battalion, and various supporting arms. Although inspired by French cavalry mechanization, these divisions were substantially weaker than the French mechanized cavalry divisions.

The windfall of Czechoslovak tanks acquired after the absorption of the Czech provinces in 1938–39 improved the equipment of the mechanized cavalry units. Prior to the start of the Polish Campaign, the 1.leichte-Division received the PzKpfw 35(t) light tanks, while the 3.leichte-Division received the more modern PzKpfw 38(t). The 2.leichte-Division was re-equipped with the PzKpfw 38(t) after the Polish campaign.

By 1938, five Panzer divisions and four light divisions had been organized. In February 1939, the general staff decided to convert the light divisions into the more versatile Panzer divisions in the autumn of 1939, but the Polish campaign intervened before this change was implemented.

The lightly armored PzKpfw I Ausf. B was especially vulnerable to mines. This particular tank with an "F" marking on the turret had been assigned to Propaganda Kompanie film crews and was knocked out near Estrées, about 10km east of Arras, where it is seen on June 6, 1940.

The initial combat use of the Panzer divisions and light divisions in Poland in September 1939 reinforced the decision to abandon the light division in favor of the Panzer divisions. In addition, the general staff agreed that the separate Panzer regiments under corps command would be incorporated into the Panzer divisions. For the France campaign, the Panzer divisions were further concentrated into corps formations, generally two Panzer divisions per corps. In the case of the main effort on the Meuse, three corps were unified under a single expedient armored group, Panzergruppe Kliest.

German tank strength, May 1940								
Unit	PzKpfw I	PzKpfw II	PzKpfw 35(t)	PzKpfw 38(t)	PzKpfw III	PzKpfw IV	Befehlspanzer	Total
1.Pz. Div.	24	115			62	48	23	272
2.Pz. Div.	24	158			86	20	*	288
3.Pz. Div.	109	122			29	20	*	280
4.Pz. Div.	160	107			44	32	23	366
5.Pz. Div.	75	116			35	32	*	258
6.Pz. Div.		50	106			26	10	192
7.Pz. Div.	37	72		48		23	*	180
8.Pz. Div.		15		180		30	*	225
9.Pz. Div.	28	72			45	11	*	156
10.Pz. Div.	66	128			48	36	*	278
Deployed strength	523	955	106	228	349	278	220	2,659
Available strength	1,077	1,092	143	238	381	290	244	3,465
Losses 5-6/40	182	240	45	54	135	97	69	822

*Complete data on command tanks not available

TECHNICAL FACTORS

Panzerkampfwagen I

In spite of the restrictions of the Versailles Treaty, Germany had begun to work on tanks in the late 1920s. Early experimental types such as the *Grosstraktor* lacked the mobility necessary for modern Panzer tactics as well as being inordinately expensive. Lutz recognized that the new Panzer divisions would require thousands of tanks, and this could not be accomplished with large and expensive designs. Furthermore, German industry was not yet ready to produce large tanks. Instead, Krupp was contracted to design a much smaller and less expensive light tank that emerged in 1934 as the Panzerkampfwagen I. The initial PzKpfw I Ausf. A weighed 5.4 tonnes and was armed with two 7.92mm machine guns. It had a two-man crew: a driver and gunner/commander. The armor basis was 13mm, enough to protect against rifle fire.

In later years, the PzKpfw I was misleadingly characterized as a mere "training tank." This was certainly not the case. By early 1930s standards, this was an efficient and well-armed design. It should be recalled that at this time, tankettes made up the bulk of tank production in most of Europe, such as the Italian L3, Polish TK or Soviet T-27. The PzKpfw I fitted comfortably into the German tank doctrine of the time as summarized in a 1936 report: "The classical role for tanks is to overcome machine guns that have dominated the battlefield, while at the same time crossing terrain obstructions. Therefore, the three primary features of the tank are protection against machine gun fire, armament of machine guns and cannon to engage targets, and high cross-

This old PzKpfw I Ausf. A was one of 51 that were modified in October 1939 as turretless *Munitionsschlepper* with a simple metal cover over the turret ring. It was serving with the 4.Panzer Division when it was put out of action in May 1940. The white air identification marking is visible on the engine deck.

country mobility with the capability to cross trenches and barbed wire."

Production of the PzKpfw I Ausf. A continued until June 1936, by which time 818 had been manufactured. Production of the PzKpfw I Ausf. B began in August 1935. This improved version used a lengthened hull and suspension with an uprated engine. A total of 675 were manufactured through June 1937. A number of sub-variants were manufactured, of which the most significant was the *kleiner Panzerbefehlswagen*, a dedicated command tank fitted with both the FuG 2 and FuG 6 radios. These were based primarily on the lengthened chassis, and a total of 184 were manufactured through 1937.

German tanks: technical characteristics						
Type	PzKpfw IB	PzKpfw IIC	Pz 35(t)	PzKpfw 38(t)	PzKpfw IIIF	PzKpfw IVD
Crew	2	3	3	3	5	5
Weight (tonnes)	5.8	8.9	10.5	9.4	19.8	20
Length (m)	4.4	4.8	4.9	4.5	5.4	5.9
Width (m)	2.1	2.2	2.1	2.1	2.9	2.8
Height (m)	1.7	2.0	2.35	2.4	2.4	2.7
Engine HP	59	138	120	123	296	296
Main armament	2 x 7.92mm	20mm	37mm	37mm	37mm	75mm
Frontal armor (mm)	13	14.5 + 20	25	25	30	30

Panzerkampfwagen II

There is only one recorded instance of tank-vs.-tank fighting in World War I, and as a result, tank doctrine in the early 1930s placed little emphasis on tank weapons capable of defeating enemy tanks. As the scale of tank production multiplied in Europe in the mid-1930s, the Wehrmacht sought a light tank capable of engaging enemy tanks. This resulted in the PzKpfw II tank that entered serial production in March 1937. This was armed with a KwK 30 20mm automatic cannon as well as a single 7.92mm machine gun. This could penetrate 14mm of armor angled at 30 degrees at 500m and 20mm of armor at 100m. This was barely adequate when compared to other light tanks of the period, such as the Soviet T-26 that had 15mm armor. It was also inadequate against newer French designs of the late 1930s, such as the Renault R 35 and Hotchkiss H 35, which had 40mm armor in the frontal areas. The decision to proceed with production of the PzKpfw II was largely due to the need for more tanks to fill out the increasing number of Panzer divisions. Larger and heavier tanks were only beginning to reach production, as detailed below.

Another important improvement to the PzKpfw II was the introduction of a third crewman to operate the tank radio. The earlier PzKpfw I had been fitted with the FuG 2, which was only a radio receiver. The PzKpfw II introduced the FuG 5, which consisted of a transmitter and receiver. The PzKpfw II underwent considerable evolution during its production run. The initial type of running-gear proved to offer poor mobility and led to a redesign that introduced larger road-wheels and a more robust spring suspension.

By 1936, the German army was beginning to have second thoughts about the wisdom of its lightly armored, weakly armed PzKpfw I and PzKpfw II tanks. There were signs that France and the Soviet Union were adopting more powerful antitank guns and tanks with heavier armor. Early in 1936, Gen Ludwig von Beck, the army chief of staff, questioned the *Waffenamt* (Weapons Department) as to why it was still purchasing the light PzKpfw I and PzKfw II. It rationalized this by stating that the units equipped only with PzKpfw Is and PzKpfw IIs "without question ... have a very significant combat value." However, in March 1936, the Waffenamt released a study on tank development that acknowledged that "in the future, lightly armored Panzers will be pinned down by heavy weapons' fire just as in the last war the infantry and cavalry were forced to ground and stymied by machine guns. Among the known enemy antitank weapons, the Waffenamt views the French 25mm Hotchkiss gun as the most important and dangerous at this time." The main reason for the continued production of light tanks was that the PzKfw III was not yet mature enough for mass production and there was a continuing demand for new tanks to fill out the new Panzer divisions.

A PzKpfw II Ausf. B of 5.Kompanie, Pz. Rgt. 7, 10.Panzer Division during exercises near Suippes, France after the summer campaign. Not all PzKpfw IIs received the upgraded front hull armor after the 1939 Polish campaign. This provides a good view of the bison insignia used by this division.

The most serious problem of the PzKpfw II in combat was revealed during the 1939 campaign in Poland. The 15mm armor could be readily penetrated by the Polish 7.92mm antitank rifles, to say nothing of 37mm antitank guns. To reduce their vulnerability, a significant portion of the PzKpfw II force was upgraded with 20mm appliqués on the front of the hull and turret prior to the Battle of France.

A trio of PzKpfw II Ausf. Cs of the regimental staff of Pz.Rgt. 25, 7.Panzer Division move over an engineer pontoon bridge erected over the Canal d'Aire near Cuinchy, May 27, 1940.

Panzerkampfwagen III

The German army's requirements for the next generation of tanks beyond the PzKpfw I were laid out by Lutz's Inspectorate for Motor Troops in 1933. These were given cover-names for secrecy – the *Zugführerwagen* (ZW: Platoon commander's vehicle) and the *Bataillonführerwagen* (BW: Battalion commander's vehicle). They would eventually emerge as the PzKpfw III and PzKpfw IV.

A PzKpfw III of 6.Kompanie, II./Pz.Rgt.36, 4.Panzer Division moves off the road near Waremme to advance cross-country during the approach march towards the Gembloux Gap on the afternoon of May 11, 1940.

A German report clarified the distinction between the two types: "The PzKpfw III is the assault tank (*Sturmwagen*), an 'armored infantryman' (*gepanzerte Infanterist*) which wins the mobile battle with the annihilating power of its machine guns. The 37mm gun has been added to deal with the threat of an armored opponent. The PzKpwfw IV is the over-watch tank (*Überwachungswagen*) following immediately behind the PzKpfw III and supporting it in overcoming the enemy. The ratio of PzKpfw III to PzKpfw IV is about the same as the infantry's ratio of light machine guns to heavy machine guns."

The general staff approved the development of the ZW/BW types in January 1934 and the Waffenamt issued the technical requirements to the industry in February 1934. Krupp was assigned to develop the turrets for both types, so they were very similar in appearance and layout. The most important innovation in both designs was the decision to employ a three-man crew in the turret. This was based on lessons learned during clandestine experiments with the Red Army at the Kama tank school in the Soviet Union in the late 1920s and early 1930s. This revealed the need for a tank commander to be free from other tasks such as loading or aiming the gun. A dedicated loader and gunner allowed the commander to concentrate on leading the tank in battle.

Large-scale production of the PzKpfw III was delayed by problems with the suspension and transmission. Ultimately, the initial chassis required a complete redesign, with the PzKpfw III Ausf. D emerging in early 1938 as the first version suitable for mass production. Only 30 were produced in 1938, as the lessons from the Spanish Civil War made it clear that its armor was inadequate against the new generation of tank and antitank guns in the 37mm–45mm range.

The German army had dispatched a small "volunteer" tank force to Spain to serve as advisers for Franco's Nationalist army. In the occasional tank-vs.-tank battles in Spain, the Republican T-26 tanks dominated the Nationalist tank units equipped with the PzKpfw I light tanks and Italian L3 tankettes.

 B

PZKPFW II IN THE BATTLE OF FRANCE

1. PzKpfw II Ausf. C, Stab, Pz.Rgt. 25, 7.Panzer Division, France, May 1940

Tanks of the brigade and regimental headquarters used tactical numbers with the prefix "R," as in this example, R12. This was sometimes repeated on the turret rear, but in this case, this was not done, and another Balkan cross was painted instead. The air identification rectangle is painted here latitudinally across the engine deck.

2. PzKpfw II Ausf. C, 1.Kompanie, Pz.Rgt. 25, 7.Panzer Division, France, May 1940

In contrast to headquarters vehicles, tanks in the companies used a three-digit tactical number with the first number indicating company, the second indicating platoon (Zug) and the third indicating the vehicle number. In the 7.Panzer Division, Pz.Rgt.25 used a large red number with white trim. The divisional insignia of the 7.Panzer Division was an inverted "Y" followed by three superscript dots, usually painted in chrome yellow. This was usually carried on the hull superstructure and was sometimes repeated on one of the rear surfaces.

1

2

The machine-gun-armed German and Italian tanks were nearly useless against the T-26, while its 45mm gun could defeat them at normal combat range.[1] In addition, tanks protected with only 15mm of frontal armor could not press home attacks against infantry defended by 37mm–45mm antitank guns. The Spanish Civil War made it clear that the lightly armed, machine-gun-armed tanks of the early 1930s were obsolete and that a new generation of gun-armed tanks with better armor was essential.

A PzKpfw III Ausf. F of I./Pz.Rgt. 1, 1.Panzer Division on the outskirts of Bouillon, Belgium during the advance over the Semois River to Sedan on May 13, 1940. The tactical number "222" indicated 2.Kompanie, 2.Zug, 2.Panzer.

A PzKpfw IV Ausf. B leads a column from the 9.Panzer Division through the town of Toussy on June 17, 1940 during the final drive into central and southern France.

The Spanish lessons led to the quick development of the PzKpfw III Ausf. E, which had 30mm armor. Lingering problems with the transmission delayed delivery of the PzKpfw III Ausf. E to December 1938. During the September 1939 war with Poland, there were 98 PzKpfw IIIs in service, consisting mainly of the pre-series types from Ausf. A through Ausf. D, with a handful of the new Ausf. E.

Production of the PzKpfw III Ausf. E ended in October 1939 after only 96 had been manufactured, switching to the modestly improved Ausf. F. The main effort was to extend PzKpfw III production to additional plants. By 1940, five more assembly plants were involved in the program besides Daimler-Benz. As a result, there were more than 380 PzKpfw III tanks available at the start of the Battle of France in May 1940.

The Waffenamt began work on a better-armed version of the PzKpfw III in January 1938, based on the obvious obsolescence of the 37mm gun to deal with newer thicker-armored British and French tanks. The potential use of a 50mm gun had been the source of bureaucratic controversy since 1936, due to the desire to maintain standardization between the PzKpfw III and the infantry's 37mm antitank gun. The 50mm tank gun would require a new family of ammunition, and some departments in the army contested such a costly and disruptive innovation. Resistance was finally overcome and development of both a new 50mm tank gun and a new 50mm antitank gun for the infantry was initiated in 1938. The PzKpfw III Ausf. G with the 50mm gun were not in service use until August 1940, so none took part in the Battle of France.

1   Steven Zaloga, *Spanish Civil War Tanks: The Proving Ground for Blitzkrieg*, Osprey New Vanguard 170, 2010.

Besides the standard PzKpfw III tanks, the Waffenamt also developed a large command tank (*grosser Pz.Bef. Wg.*) on the PzKpfw III chassis. These dispensed with the main gun to provide more space in the turret for radios. They were issued on a scale of two to the Panzer battalion headquarters, two to the Panzer regiment headquarters, three to the Panzer brigade headquarters, and seven to Panzer division headquarters, a grand total of 22 per division. The radio configurations depended on their role at battalion, regiment, or brigade level, and so had different vehicle designations (*Sonderkraftfahrzeug Sd.Kfz. 266, 267, and 268*). About 75 had been produced by the time of the Battle of France in 1940.

The PzKpfw IV Ausf. D commanded by Lt Karl Hanke of Pz.Rgt.25, with the divisional insignia of the 7.Panzer Division evident immediately in front of the Balkan cross. This tank served with Rommel's Gefechtsstaffel during the campaign in France, shielding the numerous command and radio vehicles. Hanke knocked out several French tanks and subsequently was decorated with the Iron Cross 1st and 2nd Class.

Panzerkampfwagen IV

The genesis of the PzKpfw IV was not due to concern over tank fighting, but rather the need for a more powerful tank to assist in combating field works and other enemy positions with high-explosive firepower. It was armed with a short 75mm gun, dubbed the "cigar butt" by its crews. Production of the initial PzKpfw IV Ausf. A started in October 1937 and only 35 were built before the improved Ausf. B was introduced in April 1938. Chastened by Spanish Civil War experiences, the Waffenamt ordered the frontal armor thickened to 30mm. It was followed in September 1938 by the PzKpfw IV Ausf. C, which offered modest improvements. The next major evolution became the PzKpfw IV Ausf. D, which was the definitive type used during the Battle of France. The thickness of its side armor increased from 15mm to 20mm and an external mantlet was added to better protect the main gun opening on the turret front. The hull machine gun, which had been removed from the Ausf. B and C was reintroduced on the Ausf. D. While the evolution of the PzKpfw IV saw a steady increase in armor, the German army clearly favored mobility over armored protection.

A PzKpfw IV Ausf. D of the 2.Zug, 4.Kompanie, Pz.Rgt. 1, 1.Panzer Division pushes through an orchard near Servance in the Haute-Saône department of eastern France on June 22, 1940.

By the outbreak of war on September 1, 1939, there were 211 PzKpfw IV in service. Nineteen were lost during the Polish campaign and more than 50 required an extensive overhaul due to battle damage or mechanical breakdown. The fighting in Poland showed the PzKpfw IV to be vulnerable to all modern antitank weapons, including Polish antitank rifles and the Bofors 37mm antitank gun. This resulted in the PzKpfw IV Ausf. E being fitted with 50mm frontal armor, but these updated tanks did not become available until September

1940, after the France campaign. By May 1940 at the start of the Battle of France, 290 PzKpfw IVs were available.

Czech war booty

The German annexation of the Czech provinces in March 1939 provided a windfall of tanks for the Wehrmacht. Of the various types in Czechoslovak army service, two stood out. The Škoda LT vz. 35 (Lekhý Tank vzor 35- Light Tank Model 35) was the more numerous of the types and 220 were taken into German service. These were eventually designated as the PzKpfw 35(t). It had relatively old-fashioned suspension, but was armed with a good 37mm gun. It was nicknamed sarcastically the "Skoda Super Sport" by its crews. As the newer LT vz. 38 became available, the LT vz.35 was retired as a gun tank with only 125 still in service in May 1940.

A PzKpfw 35(t) of Pz.Rgt.11, 6.Panzer Division. This was the only major unit to use this tank type in France in 1940.

The more modern Czech design was the ČKD (Českomoravská-Kolben-Daněk) LT vz. 38. Ten LT vz. 38 tanks had been completed and the remaining 140 tanks from the Czechoslovak army order were in various stages of completion. The Waffenamt recommended adopting them for service and continuing production at the ČKD plant in Prague, renamed as BMM (Böhmisch-Mährische Maschinenfabrik AG: Bohemian-Moravian Industrial Plant) after its German takeover. This tank was initially called the LTM 38 Protektorat (Leichte Tank Munster 38) and subsequently renamed as the PzKpfw III (t) due to the similarity of its armament to the PzKpfw III. Eventually, it was designated as PzKpfw 38(t). Tanks manufactured for the German army were gradually modified with German fittings such as radios, intercommunication devices, tools, and other subcomponents. Technically, the PzKpfw 38(t) fell between the PzKpfw II and PzKpfw III, having a small two-man turret like the PzKpfw II, but fitted with a 37mm gun like the PzKpfw III.

The Czech tanks came at an opportune moment for the German army, because PzKpfw III production was woefully behind schedule. The addition of several hundred tanks with 37mm guns substantially assisted in the

PZKPFW 38(T) IN THE BATTLE OF FRANCE

1. PzKpfw 38(t) Ausf. B, 6./Pz.Abt.66, 7.Panzer Division, France, June 1940

Panzer Brigade.11 directed Panzer Regiment.25 and Panzer Abteilung.66. These two formations could be distinguished by their tactical numbers, with Pz.Rgt.25 using red numbers with a white trim and Pz.Abt.66 using thinner white numbers, as seen here. The numbers in this case indicate 6.Kompanie, 1.Zug, Panzer Nr. 3. This tank was probably marked with the divisional insignia on the upper left of the front superstructure plate. It was camouflaged in the finish of Dunkelgrau Nr. 46 and Dunkelbraun Nr. 45.

2. PzKpfw 38(t) Ausf. B, II./Panzer Regiment.25, 7.Panzer Division

The tactical number II02 identifies this tank as belonging to the battalion adjutant of II.Abteilung, Pz.Rgt.25. As mentioned above, this regiment used large red numbers with white trim. This tank was probably marked with the divisional insignia on the upper left of the front superstructure plate. This particular tank was knocked out in the town of Mazinghien on May 18, 1940 when hit by a French 105mm howitzer.

1

2

PzKpfw 38(t) "I01" tank of Maj Schmidt, the battalion commander of the I.Abteilung, Pz.Rgt. 25. This tank is in the *Zugführer* (platoon leader) configuration, evident from the armored plate covering the hull machine gun opening. This was necessary to provide enough space in the hull for the Fu 2 and Fu 5 radio transceiver.

mechanization of the German cavalry. There were about 275 Czech tanks in service at the start of the war, increasing to over 380 by the time of the Battle of France.

German tank strength		
	Sep 39	**May 40**
PzKpfw I	1,445	1,077
PzKpfw II	1,223	1,092
PzKpfw III	98	381
PzKpfw IV	211	290
PzKpfw 35(t)	196	143
PzKpfw 38(t)	78	238
PzBefWg	215	244
Pz. sub-total	*3,466*	*3,465*
l. PzSpWg	718	800
s.PzSpWg	307	333
PzSpWg sub-total	*1,025*	*1,133*

Panzerjäger

A small number of Panzerjäger were in service in 1940. The more significant of these was the 4.7cm PaK(t)(Sf) auf PzKpfw I Ausf. B. As its designation implies, it consisted of a Czech 47mm antitank gun mounted on a PzKpfw I Ausf. B chassis. The first 40 were delivered in April 1940 and by May there were 100 in service. These were issued to five Heeres Panzerjäger Abteilungen in 1940 to provide a mobile tank destroyer capability.

A far larger tank destroyer was the 8.8cm (Sfl) auf Zugkraftwagen 12t, consisting of a Daimler-Benz DB10 12 tonne half-track with an armored cab, fitted with an 8.8cm Flak 18 gun on the rear. It was seen as a dual-purpose weapon, suitable for antitank defense against enemy tanks, as well as for attacking fortified bunkers. Only 25 were built and they were used by the schwere Panzerjäger-Abteilung.8 with Guderian's corps during the Battle of France.

Sturmgeschütz

Led by Erich von Manstein, the German infantry branch promoted the idea of developing self-propelled versions of their two infantry guns, the leIG 18 75mm and SiG 33 150mm guns. There was considerable resistance to this by Guderian, since it involved the use of the PzKpfw III chassis that were in very short supply for the Panzer divisions.

In spite of Guderian's opposition, the StuG III was developed in the late 1930s, mounting the 75mm infantry gun in a fixed casemate on a PzKpfw III chassis. The infantry wanted to deploy a StuG battalion in each infantry division. However, there were not any assault gun units ready in time for the 1939 invasion of Poland. Only six had been delivered by March 1940 increasing to 20 in May and 30 in June. These equipped four StuG III batteries in the Battle of France.

A Pz.Jäg. I of Heeres-Pz.Jäg.Abt. (Sfl) 670 shortly after it crossed the canal near Pommerœul, and Hensies, Belgium, to the west of Mons. There were five of these tank destroyer battalions deployed in 1940 on a scale of one per field army.

In the case of the larger 150mm infantry gun, a more slapdash solution was selected, placing it precariously on top of a turretless PzKpfw I chassis with very modest armored protection. A batch of 38 150mm sIG 33 assault guns was delivered in March 1940 and they were deployed in six companies attached to Panzer divisions.

The most powerful Panzerjäger in 1940 was the 8.8cm Flak 18(Sfl) carried on an armored version of the 18t Zugkraftwagen SdKfz 8. Nicknamed "Bufla," these were used by the schwere Panzerjäger Abteilung.8 with Panzergruppe Kleist.

A Stug III Ausf. B of Sturmgeschütz Batterie.660 that was subordinate to the 8.Panzer Division and the XV.Korps for most of the campaign in France. It was one of only three Sturmgeschütz batteries to see extensive fighting in France in 1940.

THE CAMPAIGN

Fall Gelb (Plan Yellow), the final German plan for invading France and the Low Countries, was based on a maneuver scheme developed by Erich von Manstein, the chief-of-staff of Heeresgruppe A. Previous plans had featured a revised version of the 1914 Schlieffen plan, steamrolling into Belgium and northeastern France. Manstein argued that such a maneuver was entirely predictable and would lead to a massive clash that might very well turn into another grotesque stalemate as had occurred in 1914–18. Instead, Manstein proposed that Heeresgruppe B "wave the red flag" as in a bull fight, luring the best French and British forces deep into Belgium and France. At this point, Heeresgruppe A would play the part of the matador's sword, executing a *Sichelschnitt* (Sickle Cut) through the Ardennes and thereby trapping the best Allied units against the English Channel.

Manstein's plan rested on several assessments. First, he believed that the effectiveness of the Maginot Line had convinced the Allies that the only viable invasion route into France was via Belgium. Secondly, the Ardennes had traditionally been regarded as unsuitable for rapid maneuver due to its terrain and modest road network. Consequently, the Allied defensive plan would center around the movement of their best divisions into Belgium at the start of the conflict to establish a succession of defensive barriers across key water lines. At the heart of von Manstein's plan was the operational potential of the new Panzer divisions to conduct rapid, deep attacks behind the front lines. He expected that Heeresgruppe A could quickly transit through the Ardennes before the Allies could react. The Panzers could then disgorge into the open terrain beyond Sedan, deep behind Allied lines, and use their mobility to quickly reach the Channel coast.

One of the most ungainly assault guns in German service in 1940 was the 150mm sIG 33 (Sf) auf PzKpfw I. Six companies of these were deployed in 1940, this example with sIG (Sf) Kompanie.706, 7.Panzer Division. The wicker tubes behind the gun breech were used to transport the ammunition.

The 7.Panzer Division in France was commanded by GenMaj Erwin Rommel, seen here with a PzKpfw II behind. The officer in the center is Obst Karl Rothenburg, commander of Pz.Rgt.25.

Gen Franz Halder, the chief of the army's general staff, originally opposed Manstein's scheme. A sequence of wargames and staff studies in the autumn and early winter of 1939–40 concluded that Manstein's risky scheme was Germany's only way to win a quick and decisive victory against the Allies and avoid a repeat of 1914–18.

Heeresgruppe B contained 29 infantry divisions reinforced by two Panzer divisions in Gen Erich Hoepner's LIV.Armee Korps. Due to its key role as "the matador's sword," Gen Gerd von Rundstedt's Heeresgruppe A contained the bulk of the Wehrmacht's Panzer force – seven of the ten Panzer divisions. These were organized into four corps. The most critical role would be played by von Kleist's Panzer Gruppe that contained half of the Panzer divisions. These were deployed in Guderian's XIX Armee Korps (XIX.AK) and Wietersheim's XIV.AK.

Organization of Panzer force in May 1940			
Army	**Panzer corps**	**Commander**	**Panzer divisions**
Heeresgruppe A		**GenObst Gerd von Rundstedt**	
Panzergruppe Kliest		*Gen d.Kav. Ewald von Kleist*	
	XIX.AK (mot)	Gen d.Pz. Heinz Guderian	1, 2, 10
	XLI.AK (mot)	Gen d.Pz. Georg-Hans Reinhardt	6, 8
4.Armee		*GenObst Hans-Günther von Kluge*	
	XV.AK (Mot)	Gen d.Pz Hermann Hoth	5, 7
Heeresgruppe B		**GenObst Fedor von Bock**	
18.Armee		Gen d.Art Georg von Küchler	9
	XVI.AK (Mot)	Gen d.Pz Erich Hoepner	3, 4

The Heeresgruppe B attack

Hoepner's XVI.Korps, containing the 3. and 4.Panzer Divisions, pushed into The Netherlands near Maastricht on May 10. Dutch engineers demolished the Maas (Meuse) bridges, delaying the advance for a day until German

The 150mm sIG 33 (Sf) mounted the standard heavy infantry gun on a modified PzKpfw I Ausf. B chassis with a thin armored shield around the gun. This example named "Berta" served with sIG (Sfl) Kompanie.706, 7.Panzer Division.

pioneers created tactical bridge crossings using pontoon bridges. The initial pace of the attack depended as much on skilled engineer work as on the Panzers. The first serious combat took place the next morning, on May 11, when the lead Panzer columns came under Allied air attack near the Belgian frontier. In the afternoon, the Panzer spearheads bumped into French forward scout elements including armored cars from the 3e DLM (*Division légère mécanique*: Light Mechanized Division), leading to some small skirmishes. Hoepner's mission was to push to the Gembloux Gap. This is a traditional invasion route from Germany into northeastern France via the central Belgian plain. Known in French as the *Trouée de Gembloux*, it is a natural watershed between Brussels and Namur bounded in the northwest by the Escaut (Scheldt) River and to the southeast by the Meuse (Maas). The area is flat with few natural obstacles when moving in a southwestward direction.

By the second day of the attack, the 4.Panzer Division was in the lead, about 50km from Gembloux. The 3.Panzer Division was trailing behind due to delays in crossing the Meuse River, because of road congestion and Allied air attacks on the bridge sites. Towards day's end, Hoepner gave the 4.Panzer Division its objective for May 12 – the town of Hannut.

Advancing towards Hannut from the opposite side was Gén René Prioux's Cavalry Corps, including the 2e DLM and 3e DLM. These French mechanized cavalry divisions were smaller than a Panzer division and were oriented towards traditional cavalry missions, such as reconnaissance and screening operations. They were well equipped with tanks, including the Hotchkiss H 39 and Somua S 35.

Organizational comparison, May 1940		
	3e DLM	**4.Pz.Div.**
Tank regiments	2	2
Motorized infantry battalions	3	4
Troop strength	10,446	12,340
Light tanks	163	258
Medium tanks	96	73
Tank sub-total	*259*	*331*

The mission of the Prioux Cavalry Corps was to advance into Belgium as a screening force for Gén Gaston Bilotte's *1er Groupe d'Armées* (1st Army Group). The initial assignment was to locate the advancing German forces, and once this was accomplished, the corps was to conduct blocking actions as long as possible. As in the case of Hoepner's corps, Prioux's force was also aimed at the Gembloux Gap. The lead scout element of the division reached to within 10km of Gembloux on the first day of the war.

By May 11, Prioux's advance scouts had got as far as The Netherlands, where they had encountered the lead elements of Heeresgruppe B, including the 4.Panzer Division. Prioux ordered the scouts to recoil back to their divisions where they formed a screen northwest of Gembloux, centered on the town of Hannut. The 2e DLM was assigned the right flank from Huy on the Meuse to Hannut, and the 3e DLM on the left flank from Hannut to Tirlemont. This 35km front was too wide to be defended by only two cavalry divisions. However, the mission was not rigid defense, but rather a mobile screen to delay the approaching German army until the French infantry divisions arrived on May 14.

A PzKpfw I Ausf. B and a PzKpfw II of 1./I./Pz.Rgt. 36, 4.Panzer Division move through a field between Tongeren and Waremme around noon on May 11, 1940 during the advance on the Gembloux Gap in Belgium.

The usual French cavalry practice was to create strongpoints in the towns with a squadron of mounted dragoons supported by a few Hotchkiss tanks. The farm fields between the strongpoints could be overwatched from the villages and covered by the dragoons' 25mm antitank guns. To prevent Panzer infiltration between the strongpoints, squadrons of Somua S 35 tanks were stationed a few kilometers behind, counterattacking any penetration past the line of defended towns.

The world's first great tank battle

The first large tank battle in world history took place over the next few days during a clash between Hoepner's and Prioux's corps in the vicinity of Hannut. More than a thousand tanks were involved on both sides. On the morning of May 12, lead elements of Pz.Rgt.35 of the 4.Panzer Division began skirmishing with the 2e Cuirassiers of the 3e DLM around Hannut. Hptm Ernst Freiherr von Jungenfeld, company commander of 6./Pz.Rgt. 35, later recalled in his memoirs that the fighting was "hard and bloody; many a brave Panzermann had to lay down his life for the Fatherland. Many were wounded and a large number of tanks were lost, in part to enemy fire and in part to breakdowns."

A light tank company of I./Pz.Rgt.36, 4.Panzer Division in the fields outside Gembloux in mid-May 1940. The tank in the foreground, "136," is a PzKpfw I Ausf. B, with earlier PzKpfw I Ausf. A tanks evident in front of it.

Although the 4.Panzer Division was ordered to proceed to Gembloux that afternoon, by this stage of the battle, it had run out of fuel. The situation was so critical that the Luftwaffe was ordered to airdrop special rubber fuel bladders, delivering 30,000 liters in two missions. This allowed the division to stage a raid around dusk to make inroads into the French defenses. The first day's fighting finally ended around nightfall. French losses during the day were 24 Hotchkiss and 4 Somua tanks.

The commander of Pz.Rgt. 36, 4.Panzer Division, Obst Kurt von Jesser on Befehlspanzer Ausf. F "RN1" south of Gembloux on May 17, 1940. The tactical number indicated the *Nachrichten Zug* (Signals Platoon) of the regimental headquarters. The small dot after RN1 indicated Pz.Rgt.36; Pz.Rgt.35 lacked the dot.

Hoepner's corps made little progress on May 12, both due to the clashes between the 4.Panzer Division and 3e DLM, as well as the slow arrival of the 3.Panzer Division. The 6.Armee commander, GenObst von Reichenau, was infuriated at the slow pace of the 3.Panzer Division and visited its headquarters to get it moving faster. The delays were caused by a combination of traffic congestion and Allied air attacks on the Meuse bridges. By nightfall, 3.Panzer Division began to arrive on the northern flank of 4.Panzer Division in the vicinity of Hannut. Hoepner had great hopes for the following day, since he had both Panzer divisions ready to attack towards Gembloux. Gén Bougrain, leading the 2e DLM, wanted to intervene against the Panzers around Hannut, but Prioux told him to keep his division in screening positions to deal with the German infantry divisions advancing from the Liège area. As a result, the fighting on May 13 near Hannut would pit two Panzer divisions against the 3e DLM.

The fighting on May 13 got off to a slow start. Hoepner wanted to soften up French positions with airstrikes, but the VIII Fliegerkorps would not be ready to attack until 1100hrs, further delaying the start of the attack. The Panzer tactics differed between divisions. The fresh 3.Panzer Division, attacked with both of its Panzer regiments in the lead, followed by a rifle battalion behind each Panzer regiment. In contrast, the 4.Panzer Division attacked with the riflemen in the lead, with plans to pass the Panzer regiments through the gaps for exploitation once the French defenses had been penetrated. Hoepner's XVI.Korps had about 560 tanks available at the start of the day's attack.

Based on the previous day's fighting, the 4.Panzer Division was well aware of the difficulty of dealing with the heavily armored French tanks, and so brought forward the division's 88mm Flak guns and PzKpfw IV tanks. The 88mm guns remained at stand-off range and attempted to engage any Somua that could be spotted near the town. The PzKpfw IV accompanied the infantry towards its objectives. Jungenfeld later described the advance as "devilishly difficult." By mid-afternoon, the Panzers were low on ammunition, and some of the light tanks broke off to return to the

rear areas to secure more 37mm and 75mm ammunition for the essential PzKpfw III and PzKpfw IV tanks.

The afternoon fighting forced the French to conduct a contested withdrawal. By mid-afternoon of May 13, the 3e DLM had exhausted its reserves. The two days of fighting on May 12–13 cost the 3e DLM a total of 105 Hotchkiss and Somua tanks of the original 250. Hoepner's corps started the campaign with a total of 674 Panzers, with about 560 ready for action on May 13. This suggests that over 110 tanks were lost or were under repair after the initial fighting on May 10–12. French accounts claim that 164 Panzers were knocked out on May 12–13. The fighting petered out late in the day with both sides low on ammunition and fuel.

D **BATTLE FOR THE GEMBLOUX GAP: "THE WITCHES' CAULDRON" MAY 13, 1940**

Hoepner's XVI.Korps, including the 3. and 4.Panzer Divisions, was tasked with pushing through the Gembloux Gap in Belgium as the northern element of the Wehrmacht's "Sickle Cut" to trap advanced Allied forces. On the French side, Prioux's Cavalry Corps, consisting of the 2e and 3e DLM (*Divisions légères mécaniques*: light mechanized divisions) was assigned as a mobile screening force that would race into Belgium and establish a preliminary defensive line. The corps was expected to hold this line for a few days to give the follow-up force of French infantry divisions enough time to move up into Belgium. Hoepner's and Prioux's forces began to clash in a series of violent engagements in Belgium, from May 11, 1940.

These clashes reached a peak of intensity on May 13 when 4.Panzer Division clashed with elements of the 3e DLM in the fields between Jandrain and Jauche. The advancing Panzers were brought under intense French artillery fire while fighting against French Hotchkiss 39H and Somua 35S tanks. The fields were remembered by German Panzer troops as the "witches' cauldron" due to the violence of the encounter.

Pz.Rgt.35 deployed its PzKpfw IV tanks in the vanguard, since their 75mm guns were the only tank guns powerful enough to deal with the French defensive positions located in the villages of the area. The German Panzer crews had quickly learned that the French cavalry tanks were not particularly vulnerable to any of their guns, except for the 75mm guns of the PzKpfw IV. After hours of fighting, the French defenders in Jandrin were ordered to fall back west to Jauche, since it was threatened with encirclement by the advance of 3.Panzer Division from the north. Fighting stopped later in the day as both sides were low on ammunition and fuel. Two more days of fighting were needed before Hoepner's corps was able to advance through the Gembloux Gap.

Pz.Rgt.1 of the 1.Panzer Division used improvised armored ambulances based on the PzKpfw I Ausf. B, such as the one seen here on May 14, 1940 while crossing the Meuse River. French prisoners are being escorted to the opposite side.

During the night of May 13–14, Hoepner's headquarters believed that the French defenses had been overcome and that the next day would finally start the exploitation phase of the campaign with deep advances to the French frontier. Despite the Luftwaffe's command of the air, there was little appreciation that the French were establishing their main defense line in the Gembloux Gap and that they had simply pushed back the cavalry screening force. In the early morning hours of May 14, both Panzer divisions began to advance towards the fixed antitank barrier at Perwez. Skirmishing with the French cavalry tanks continued through the morning. By the afternoon, the Panzer divisions' spearheads had been stopped by French defensive strongpoints on either side of the town of Gembloux and by unexpectedly heavy artillery fire. This artillery fire came from the French infantry divisions which had recently arrived in the area. With their screening mission accomplished, Prioux's cavalry corps was instructed to pull back behind the French infantry defenses in the afternoon.

At first, Heeresgruppe B did not appreciate that the opposing French forces had dramatically changed from a thin screen of French mechanized cavalry to a much denser infantry defense. Hoepner's corps was instructed to push through the "defeated enemy" around Gembloux. Pressured into attacking on May 15 before supporting German infantry divisions could arrive, the attacks by Hoepner's two Panzer divisions on May 15 were a complete failure. The 4.Panzer Division surgeon recalled in his diary that the fighting for Gembloux on May 15 had been a "very black day." Casualties that day were 547 men, more than the previous five days of fighting combined.

By the end of May 15, Hoepner's Panzer divisions were exhausted. The 3.Panzer Division had had 20–25 percent of its tanks knocked out or in repair and 4.Panzer Division had only 137 tanks functional by day's end out of its original 331 Panzers. As of May 25, total tank losses were 42 in 3.Panzer Division and 51 in 4.Panzer Division, though many more Panzers were inoperative due to combat damage or mechanical problems. The Panzer divisions' rifle regiments were in especially bad shape. One battalion from Schützen Regiment.12 was down to 4 officers and 31 men from an initial strength of 700. The 4.Panzer Division headquarters informed Hoepner that the division could not be expected to take part in the planned attack scheduled for May 16. On the French side, the 1re Division Marocaine had borne the brunt of the attacks by the two Panzer divisions and had suffered nearly 2,000 casualties, or about a quarter of its strength.

The French were finally forced to withdraw from the Gembloux Gap, due to the success of Manstein's bold "Sickle-Cut" maneuver through the Ardennes behind them to the south. With the bulk of the Panzer divisions streaming across the Meuse River near Sedan, the French 1re Armée was obliged to withdraw, fighting a bloody two-week rearguard action that ended at Dunkirk.

In the end, both sides claimed victory in the four-day Battle for the Gembloux Gap. The French army had won a tactical victory at both Hannut and Gembloux. Prioux's cavalry corps had fulfilled its mission of delaying Hoepner's Panzers long enough for the 1re Armée to establish a firm defensive line in the Gembloux Gap. With its mission accomplished, the cavalry corps withdrew in good order. From the German perspective, the Battle for the Gembloux Gap was an operational success. The intention of Heeresgruppe B was to lure the best French and British divisions into Belgium, catching them in a sack once Heeresgruppe A thrust out of the Ardennes. The presence of Hoepner's XVI.Korps masked the fact that most of the German Panzer force was elsewhere, distracting Allied high command from the location and timing of the main blow.

A PzKpfw IV Ausf. D leads a column from the 2.Panzer Division past Hôtel à la Glycine in Vresse-sur-Semois, Belgium on May 12, 1940. This division continued to use the 1930s style of small rhomboid insignia evident on the lower bow plate rather than the large tactical numbers adopted in many other Panzer divisions.

A PzKpfw II Ausf. C of the Nachrichten Zug (Signals Platoon) of Pz.Rgt. 4, 2.Panzer Division in the village of Sugny on May 13, 1940 during the advance on Sedan.

"The Matador's Sword": Guderian at Sedan

The role of "The Matador's Sword" was carried out by Panzergruppe Kleist, which consisted of Guderian's XIX.Korps with three Panzer divisions and Reinhardt's XLI.Korps with two Panzer divisions. Guderian's corps had the most vital mission of rapidly breaching the French defenses on the Meuse River near Sedan.

The advance through the Ardennes took nearly four days from May 10 to May 13. Although there was some skirmishing with Belgian forces, the

A PzKpfw IV Ausf. D "711" of 7. Pz.Rgt. 8, 10.Panzer Division, knocked out on the outskirts of Stonne by a 25mm antitank gun of the 67e Régiment d'Infanterie on May 15, 1940. This was the start of a bitter battle for the town, later called the "Verdun of 1940" by German participants.

main impediment to the German advance was the inadequate road network and the corresponding traffic congestion. The actual attack on Sedan had been meticulously planned in March 1940 during a series of wargames. The Luftwaffe began the assault on May 13 with a day-long series of rolling attacks to destroy French bunkers and other defenses near the crossing sites along the Meuse and to demoralize the French defenders. The river crossings were conducted by infantry with engineer support using inflatable assault boats. The focal point of the attack was in the 1.Panzer Division sector with the 2.Panzer Division and 10.Panzer Division on either side. The 1.Panzer Division had the most favorable route and crossing site immediately to the west of Sedan.

The French defenses in the Sedan sector consisted of a reserve French infantry division, deployed in prepared defenses and bunkers with ample machine-gun and artillery support. Although elements of the French division near the crossing point put up a spirited defense, the division was inadequately trained and thoroughly demoralized by the prolonged Luftwaffe air strikes. Many of the initial German river crossings were repulsed, but by nightfall, the Germans had a firm foothold over the Meuse in all three divisional sectors. German engineers frantically attempted to erect a bridge near Gaulier to allow the Panzers to pass over to the west bank. By the morning of May 14, 4.Kompanie, Pz.Rgt.2 was the only armored unit that had crossed the river.

The Allies responded on May 14 with a series of desperate air attacks on the German bridges. The Luftwaffe had anticipated this response and the French and British air strikes were repulsed with heavy losses caused by German fighters and Flak. On the ground, the French X Corps ordered several infantry divisions along with associated infantry tank battalions to counterattack the crossing sites to block the German advance.

The first tank action in this sector began on the morning of May 14 near Bulson. The French defense at Bulson included infantry regiments supported by the 4e and 7e BCC (*Bataillons des char de combat*), equipped with the

E

PZKPFW III IN THE BATTLE OF FRANCE

1. PzKpfw III Ausf. F, 6./Panzer-Regiment.35, 4.Panzer Division, Belgium, May 1940

This was the tank of the 6.Kompanie commander, Htpm Ernst Freiherr von Jungenfeld. He was famous in Germany for a set of reminiscences of his adventures as a young man in South America published in 1916. In his company, he was nicknamed "Unser Pampas" (Our Pampas) for his exploits in Paraguay. As a result, he had the name "Pampas" painted in large letters on his tank.

2. PzKpfw III Ausf. F, 5./Panzer-Regiment.7, 10.Panzer Division, Belgium, May 1940

Panzer Regiment.7 had a unique insignia, a bison painted on the turret side and rear. This was created by placing a stencil of the bison on the turret and then airbrushing around the edge of the silhouette in white. The 5.Kompanie carried its insignia as a large white "5" on the turret side and rear adjacent to the bison. The divisional insignia was carried on the rear on a black panel along with the tank number in chrome yellow. The tank number was painted on the hull side rather than being carried on the old-pattern metal plaque.

1

2

A PzKpfw 38(t) Ausf. B of 2./I./ Pz.Rgt.25, 7.Panzer Division, knocked out during the Arras battle with French and British forces on May 27, 1940. The grave of the tank commander, Lt Paul Lauterbach, is to the left.

best of the French infantry tanks, the FCM 36. On the German side, the 1.Panzer Division began feeding individual tank companies into the attack once it crossed the Meuse bridge. The first Panzer company to arrive was shot to pieces by 25mm infantry antitank guns. The FCM 36 proved to be very resistant to German tank fire, but its 37mm gun was equipped primarily with high-explosive projectiles that were nearly useless against the Panzers. The tide gradually turned as more German Panzer companies arrived on the scene. By the end of the day, the 7e BCC had lost 29 of its 37 FCM tanks; the 4e BCC saw little combat that day.

The fighting on May 14 cemented the German positions over the Meuse at Sedan. More and more Panzers flowed out of the narrow bridgehead. Guderian had been instructed to wait until sufficient infantry divisions had secured the Meuse bridgehead before plunging westward with the Panzer divisions. He ignored these instructions in order to exploit the confusion in the Allied command and sent both 1.Panzer Division and 2.Panzer Division in a race to the Channel. Guderian's immediate worry was the Mont-Dieu plateau, south of the Meuse crossing sites, which could threaten the bridgehead if occupied by French troops. He expected that the French would stage their counterattack towards Sedan from Mont-Dieu, and indeed such an operation was already under way. As a result, 10.Panzer Division and Infanterie-Regiment Großdeutschland (IRGD) were assigned the task of seizing and holding the Mont-Dieu plateau to counter this threat. This led to the first major armored clash after the Meuse crossing.

The mission of crushing the Meuse bridgehead was handed to Gén J. Flavigny's 21e Corps d'Armée, which included one of the French armored divisions, the 3e DCr (*Division cuirasée*). The first elements of Flavigny's force to reach Mont-Dieu were the 6e GRDI (*Groupe de reconnaissance d'infanterie*), the divisional reconnaissance element of the 3e DIM (*Division d'infanterie motorisée*), followed by one of the infantry battalions. They established a defensive position in Stonne, the main town on the plateau.

Rommel's 7.Panzer Division engaged several French armored formations on its approach to Arras on May 17. This jumble of vehicles on the eastern outskirts of Le Cateau-Cambrésis includes a PzKpfw 38 (t) "612" of 6./Pz.Rgt.25, a Panhard P 178 armored car of the 1re Division Légère Mécanique, and Char B1 Bis "Indochine" of the 15e BCC, 2e Division Cuirassée.

The German attack on Stonne began on the morning of May 15. It was led by a battalion from the Großdeutschland Regiment, with a platoon of PzKpfw IV tanks of the 10.Panzer Division leading the way. The German tank column was decimated by the French antitank guns, but the momentum of the attack helped the German infantry take the town. The French infantry set up defensive positions outside the town and was soon joined by a company of Hotchkiss H 39 tanks of the 45e BCC that staged an immediate counterattack. Although they managed to push into the town, the light tanks lacked infantry support and were eventually forced to withdraw. They were followed by three Char B1 bis tanks that attempted to silence the German infantry's 37mm antitank guns.

This was followed by a coordinated French tank-infantry attack involving a few H 39s from the 45e BCC, a few FCM 36s from the 4e BCC, three Char B1 bis of 49e BCC, and two battalions of French infantry. The French lost five tanks in the attack, but they managed to push Großdeutschland out of Stonne. The Luftwaffe staged a Ju-87 Stuka attack on the town followed by heavy artillery, forcing the French infantry to withdraw. But the Germans were in no position to re-occupy the ruins. The fighting around Stonne had badly dispersed the 3e DCr and Flavigny's plan for a major counterattack on the Sedan bridgehead petered out. Instead, fighting for Stonne continued with a fresh tank attack on the town on the morning of May 16. Two companies of Char B1 bis tanks of 41e BCC led the attack, and one of the company commanders, Capt Billotte,

A PzKpfw I Ausf. B of 8.Kompanie, Pz.Rgt.36, 4.Panzer Division near Englefontaine, about 10km east of Cambrai, May 21, 1940.

charged into Stonne and knocked out a column of 13 Panzers in the confines of the town. Stonne changed hands no fewer than 17 times in two days of intense fighting on May 15–16.

The tank fighting for Stonne petered out after the evening of May 16. The 10.Panzer Division was pulled out and replaced by two infantry divisions; likewise the Char B1 bis battalions were withdrawn for actions in other sectors. Tank casualties were about 25 Panzers and 33 French tanks, but the infantry bore the brunt of the casualties. The fighting for Stonne was often called the "Verdun of 1940" due to its intensity. The main significance of the battle for Stonne was that it derailed the French attempts to counterattack the German bridgeheads over the Meuse near Sedan.

Pursuit to the Channel

As well as the breakthrough of Guderian's corps, other Panzer divisions had breached the Meuse. Reinhardt's XLI.Korps included the 6.Panzer Division and 8.Panzer Division. GenMaj Werner Kempf's 6.Panzer Division had failed in its original attempts to cross the Meuse at Monthermé on May 13–14, and as a result, the 12.Armee threatened to pull Reinhardt's corps back into reserve and substitute infantry divisions for the river crossing operations. Spurred on by this threat, the 6.Panzer Division pushed over the Meuse in the early morning hours of May 15, and was soon advancing deep behind French lines. Kempf organized a pursuit detachment to race ahead of the division, and it advanced 55km to Montcornet by nightfall. At this point, it was farther west than Guderian's Panzers.

To the north, Hoth's XV.Korps had pushed beyond Dinant with the 5.Panzer Division and Rommel's 7.Panzer Division. The 5.Panzer Division was the first over the Meuse near Houx in Belgium. Both of Hoth's Panzer divisions began advancing out of the bridgehead on May 14. During the morning of May 15, both divisions encountered the 1re DCr near Flavion, immobile due to the disruption in its fuel supply. In the ensuing melee, the 1re DCr and the nearby 6e BCC lost more than 140 tanks. Hoth's Panzers had managed to overrun the intended defense line of the French 9e Armée before it had even coalesced.

On May 16–17, Guderian's, Reinhardt's, and Hoth's Panzer corps advanced largely unopposed towards the Channel. The French army had not anticipated such a massive breakthrough and was unable to react quickly enough. The 9e Armée holding the Meuse front was largely dispersed or overrun. The pace of the advance was so swift that the Panzergruppe Kleist headquarters attempted to rein in Guderian's corps, fearing that they were running into a trap. The halt

Rommel's 7.Panzer Division reached the English Channel on June 10 at Les Petites-Dalles, between Dieppe and Le Havre. The cliffs here were made famous by Claude Monet's 1884 paintings. The first tank to reach the sea was B01, the Panzerbefehlswagen Ausf. E being used at the time by the Pz.Rgt.25 commander, Obst Karl Rothenburg.

Pz.Rgt.25 in La Grand Vallée on the western side of the Somme River north of Hangest-sur-Somme on June 5, 1940. To the right is a PzKpfw IV Ausf. D, while the remainder of the tanks are PzKpfw 38(t)s, the signature type of the regiment.

order had in fact come from Rundstedt's Heeresgruppe A, not on Kleist's own initiative. This dispute led to a confrontation between Kleist and Guderian at Montcornet. Guderian refused to halt his corps, at which point Kleist relieved him of his command, replacing him with GenLt Rudolf Veiel of the 2.Panzer Division. That afternoon, GenObst Wilhelm List, commander of 12.Armee, attempted to rectify the command crisis and reinstated Guderian. Guderian took this as a sign that his race to the Channel could continue.

However, the Moncornet halt order was only a symptom of growing unease in the senior German command about the excessive pace of the Panzers westward and the threat of a major flank attack from the Allies. On May 17, Hitler himself ordered the Panzers to go no farther west than Le Cateau-Laon. The Führer was afraid that a careless race westward would allow the French to achieve another "Miracle on the Marne" as they had done in 1914 when they had stopped a similar rapid German breakthrough at the gates of Paris. This halt lasted through May 18. Some divisional commanders tried to ignore the orders. Rommel pushed the 7.Panzer Division to Avesnes on the night of May 16–17, confronting French tanks including elements of the 1re DCr. While Rommel might have been court-martialed for such insubordination, it was hard to argue with his startling success and he was instead awarded the Knight's Cross.

In the midst of the halt order, the Allies made feeble attempts to stem the German tide. The partially formed 4eme DCr under the command of Col Charles de Gaulle attempted a counterattack against the 1.Panzer Division near Montcornet, but he was halted by a Panzer attack and the intervention of Ju-87 Stuka dive-bombers. When no major Allied counterattack materialized, Hitler rescinded his halt order on May 19.

With Rommel in the lead, Hoth's Panzer corps pushed out of Avesnes to the south of Arras on May 21 aiming for bridges over the Scarpe River. The division's Panzers formed the spearhead, and the 7.Panzer Division's rifle regiments followed behind with no tank support. In the afternoon, the 2./SR.7 was hit by a British force consisting of 151 Brigade supported

A Panzer attack by I./Pz.Abt.25, 7.Panzer Division during the fighting towards the Somme in early June 1940. The PzKpfw 38(t) Ausf. C in the foreground is marked "I01" indicating the tank of Maj Schmidt, the battalion commander of the I.Abteilung, Pz.Rgt. 25.

A column of PzKpfw II Ausf. B of Pz.Rgt. 1, 1.Panzer Division races over the Saône River bridge near Le Quitteur at 1630hrs on June 15, 1940 shortly after the French managed to demolish a German engineer bridge nearby.

by 4 RTR and 7 RTR equipped with Matilda infantry tanks. The 37mm PaK 36 antitank guns accompanying the German infantry were largely useless against the British tanks, especially the Matilda II that had 80mm frontal armor. The neighboring motorized column from I./SR.6 was hit by 4 RTR. The momentum of the British attack pushed farther south into the rear elements of SS-Totenkopf Division.

Fortunately for the 7.Panzer Division's infantry, the divisional artillery was nearby and began engaging the British tanks with its 105mm LFH 18 field howitzers. While these were not dedicated antitank weapons, both their high-explosive and armor-piercing rounds could do significant damage to tanks. Rommel himself appeared on the scene near Hill 111 and began directing the countermeasures. He ordered the divisional Flak including both 20mm and 88mm guns, to create a second defensive line to prevent further British penetrations. Air support arrived around 1800hrs, but by then the British attack had largely spent its energy. Of the 88 British tanks taking part in the Arras battle, 60 had been knocked out, had broken down or were abandoned. The German infantry took the heaviest losses of the campaign so far with the two battalions suffering more than 300 men killed, wounded, and missing. Pz.Rgt.25 was ordered to return towards Arras, but it became engaged in a fight with elements of the 3e DLM that was covering the British western flank.

The Battle of Arras on May 21 was one of the few successful Allied counterattacks of the campaign. It highlighted the continuing difficulty of conducting coordinated Allied operations. At a tactical level, it was a Pyrrhic victory for the British Expeditionary Force in view of the exceptionally high tank losses. On the other hand, it had substantial operational consequences. Rommel had exaggerated the threat posed to his division, sometimes claiming he had been attacked by five divisions. This exacerbated the anxiety of Hitler and many senior German commanders over the threat posed by Allied flank attacks. As a result, there was another halt of the Panzer divisions late on May 21. This prevented the forward Panzer divisions from immediately taking the Channel ports of Boulogne, Dunkirk, and Calais that were in reach. Instead, Boulogne would not fall until May 25 and Calais on May 26, since in the intervening time, the Allies had managed to solidify their defensive screen at Dunkirk. Although Arras slowed the German advance, by the third week of May, the Allied forces were disorganized and demoralized.

Planning was under way to evacuate British and French forces via the port of Dunkirk. The May 21 halt order was rescinded less than a day later, on May 22, and the Panzers again continued their advance to the coast.

By May 24, the lead Panzer divisions were forming a cordon about 15km around Dunkirk and had already leapt the last natural barrier, the Aa Canal. To the relief of the Allies, the Panzers unexpectedly halted. Again, it was the senior German commanders who had promulgated the halt order, ultimately with Hitler's consent. The two army group commanders, von Kluge and Rundstedt, both favored a temporary halt to let the infantry divisions catch up to the Panzer spearheads. The Panzer corps and Panzer division commanders, as well as the OKH (Army High Command), wanted to vigorously press forward the attack, since they had seen at first hand the perilous state of the Allied forces. Eventually Hitler and the OKW (Wehrmacht High Command) sided with the army group commanders.

The halt lasted until May 26 when Berlin finally realized its mistake. The Allied forces were able to restrain the German advance on Dunkirk until June 4, by which time about 370,000 troops had been evacuated.

Panzer status on June 8, 1940							
	PzKpfw I	PzKpfw II	PzKpfw III	PzKpfw IV	kl.Bef.	gr.Bef.	Total
3.Panzer Division							
Deployed on May 10	117	129	42	26	19	10	**343**
Total loss	31	29	10	6	1	5	**82**
Under repair	28	32	6	4	7	2	**79**
Operational June 8	58	68	26	16	11	3	**182**
Percent operational	49%	52%	62%	61%	58%	30%	**53%**
4.Panzer Division							
Deployed on May 10	141	111	40	24	6	9	**331**
Total loss	33	23	8	8	3	2	**77**
Under repair	34	25	6	1	0	1	**67**
Operational June 8	74	63	26	15	3	6	**187**
Percent operational	52%	57%	65%	63%	50%	67%	**56%**

June 4: the balance sheet

The fighting from the start of the campaign on May 10 through the final day of the Dunkirk evacuation on June 4 cost the Allies about 3,000 armored vehicles. As will be discussed later, the number of combat losses versus tanks abandoned due to fuel exhaustion or mechanical problems is not certain, but it may have been less than half of the total of the losses.

French losses totaled about 1,870 tanks, not counting the obsolete Renault FT, plus a further 390 armored cars. The losses were by far the heaviest in mechanized cavalry units, since they had raced forward into Belgium and served in the costly delaying actions against Heeresgruppe B. French cavalry units lost about 1,405 tanks and armored cars, or about 80 percent of their initial strength. In contrast, the armored divisions and infantry tank battalions had lost about 855 tanks or about 45 percent of their starting strength. The problem was not only the enormous scale of the losses, but their quality. These units constituted most of the best-equipped and best-trained French cavalry units.

"Pioniere nach vorne!" The Brückenleger II was a bridge-laying tank on the PzKpfw II, with three completed in 1939. They served with the Panzer-Pionier-Bataillon.58 (mot) of the 7.Panzer Division in France in 1940 and are seen here during the fighting along the Somme in June 1940. Behind the lead Brückenleger are a pair of Ladungsleger, a version of the PzKpfw I designed to deliver demolition charges from a rear-mounted frame.

British losses were about 465 armored vehicles consisting of 308 tanks and 44 armored cars of the British Expeditionary Force plus 113 tanks of the 1st Armoured Division lost at Calais and Abbeville. Belgian losses were about 50 tanks and 237 T.13 tank destroyers. Allied personnel losses were enormous with nearly 1.2 million captured.

As a consequence of these heavy losses, the Allied tank force post-Dunkirk was much smaller. The French army still had about 1,875 AFVs including 340 cavalry tanks, 140 armored cars, 270 D2s and B1 bis battle tanks, and 1,135 infantry tanks, not counting the obsolete Renault FT.

Determining German strength at this point is difficult. German total losses in May were 604 tanks and 114 armored cars. In terms of tanks, this was about 23 percent of their starting strength. However, this figure does not include vehicles inoperable due to combat damage or mechanical problems. The number of vehicles in repair was probably similar to the total losses, about 600 tanks. The number of operable Panzers on June 4 was probably about half the starting strength, or around 1,300 tanks. Reinforcements began to arrive only in early June with over 200 reserve tanks arriving in France from German depots. Panzergruppe Kleist received a resupply of 239 armored vehicles during the entire campaign. The strength of the Panzer divisions at the end of the campaign varied wildly. For example, in XVI.A.K., 3.Pz.Div. had 230 Panzers, 4.Pz.Div. had 230, but 10.Pz.Div. had only 130, and 9.Pz.Div. only 60.

While the overall strength of the Panzer divisions in early June was smaller than the size of the opposing French force, much of the French tank strength was in newly formed and inexperienced units, or units located away from the fighting front, significantly undermining their actual combat power.

Fall Rot

Following the Dunkirk evacuation, the Wehrmacht began a campaign to defeat the remainder of the French army by pushing south. This campaign was codenamed *Fall Rot* (Case Red). The conduct of this campaign was clearly in Germany's favor, since by this time, the French army numbered only 66 divisions compared to Germany's 104 divisions plus 19 in reserve. Nevertheless, the campaign was more bitterly fought than is oftentimes realized.

The French army had established the Weygand Line along the natural defenses of the Somme and Aisne rivers. Initial attacks against these defenses were frustrated by French resistance. However, in other sectors, the German advance was both swift and consequential. Rommel's 7.Panzer Division began its race towards Normandy and the port of Cherbourg. Guderian's newly enlarged Panzergruppe headed along France's eastern frontier towards the Swiss border, arriving there on June 17. Paris was declared an open city and the 18.Armee marched into the capital on June 14. This was an enormous psychological blow to the French army. Heeresgruppe C crossed the Rhine into Alsace at the old fortress city of Breisach, making contact with Guderian's advance guard at Belfort. This created a massive encirclement of nearly a half million French troops in Lorraine. On June 17, the newly appointed prime minster, Marshal Henri Pétain, requested an armistice that was signed on June 22 ending the conflict.

BATTLE ANALYSIS

The bold use of Panzer divisions was central to the German victory over France in 1940. In contrast, the performance of the French armored formations was very disappointing. The traditional explanation for this discrepancy has been the concentration of Panzers in the ten Panzer divisions. In contrast, the French army dispersed its tanks in "penny packets" between the armored divisions, mechanized cavalry divisions, and infantry tank battalions. This view was first promulgated by Basil Liddell Hart after the war. Yet the French organization was fairly similar to US and Soviet armor deployment in 1944–45. The Wehrmacht itself steadily moved away from the intense concentration of its Panzers as the war progressed, with about half

Officers of I./Pz.Rgt. 1 gather around the PzKpfw IV Ausf. A command tank "I01" of ObstLt Wilhelm Koppenburg about 1600hrs on June 19, 1940 outside Belfort during the advance of 1.Panzer Division to the Swiss border. Koppenburg is the figure immediately in front of the motorcycle dispatch rider.

of its armored fighting vehicles in the Panzer divisions by 1944 with the rest supporting the infantry. This outdated explanation is still widely held despite evidence to the contrary.

A more plausible explanation was the combat experience of the German units compared with the inexperience, lack of training, and incomplete mobilization of the French armored units. Nine of Germany's large, mechanized formations were organized by 1939 and saw combat in Poland in 1939. In contrast, only two of France's armored divisions were organized by 1939, and many of its infantry tank units were not formed until months before the outbreak of the 1940 campaign. The earlier establishment of the German formations provided more time for training. Combat experience helped to iron out tactical and logistical problems. The success of the Panzer divisions in 1940 had as much to do with the "soft" factors such as training, communications, tactics, and logistics as it had to do with the "hard" ones, such as tank design and the number of tanks.

For example, the Panzer units first became aware of the challenges of refueling tank units during an advance from their movement into Austria during the Anschluss of March 1938. Steps were taken to address this issue by the time of the Polish campaign. During the 1940 campaign, Panzers were fitted with a rack on the engine deck to carry five or six jerrycans of gasoline, providing 25–30 gallons of additional fuel. While this might seem like a minor feature, it proved invaluable during the advance through the Ardennes in the opening days of the campaign. Divisional fuel trucks became trapped in long traffic jams. With a reserve of gasoline on board, the Panzers could refuel themselves and keep advancing until the fuel trucks could catch up. In contrast, the French formations had no practical experience in conducting sustained advances. Refueling procedures were time-consuming and debilitating. The French army had excellent refueling vehicles, but production was behind schedule and many units had not received their intended complement. On repeated occasions, German Panzer formations caught French armored units stalled while refueling, such as the 1re DCr facing Hoth's Panzer corps near Flavion in mid-May 1940. The 3e DCr was so late in its creation that it lacked most of its specialized fueling vehicles. The same fate undermined de Gaulle's partially formed 4e DCr. The fueling issue was not the only problem of the French armored force, but rather it was a reflection of broader shortcomings inherent in the units' lack of experience and training.

PZKPFW IV IN THE BATTLE OF FRANCE

1. PzKpfw IV Ausf. D, 2.Panzer Division, Belgium, May 1940

This PzKpfw IV Ausf. D displays the austere markings of 2.Panzer Division, consisting of a chrome yellow rhomboid followed by the company number, with the divisional insignia of two dots below. No three-digit tactical number is evident.

2. PzKpfw IV Ausf. D, 7./II./Panzer Regiment 8, 10.Panzer Division, Stonne, France, May 1940

Pz.Rgt.8 carried its insignia, a Wolfsangel, on the turret rear. Above this was the Zug (platoon) marking. In the I.Abteilung, the stripes were vertical, while in the II.Abteilung, as is the case here, they were horizontal. The number of stripes identified the Zug, so in this case, 3.Zug. The tactical numbering pattern in Pz.Rgt.8 was unusual in that the number was carried towards the rear of the hull side and was repeated on the rear. Also, this unit did not use the usual numbering pattern with the second number identifying the Zug. Instead, the first number identified the company and the next two numbers were issued sequentially. So 700 was the company commander, 701 the company adjutant, etc.

1

2

The crew of PzKpfw IV Ausf. D "323" of Pz.Rgt.25 pose in front of their tank. The officer in the center is the tank commander, Lt Karl Hanke. He was a high-ranking Nazi party official associated with Goebbels' propaganda ministry. Although he served closely with Rommel in France, he was later dismissed by him for trying to bully other officers because of his party rank.

Although the Panzer divisions were significantly better prepared for combat than their French opponents, there were tactical issues that needed attention. German combined-arms tactics were still immature. The lack of tracked infantry vehicles hindered Panzer/infantry tactics and the Panzer regiments and infantry regiments still tended to fight their own battles in 1940. A good example of this problem was the battle of Arras between Rommel's 7.Panzer Division and British tank units. The 2./Schützen Regiment.7 was operating on its own when struck by British tanks on May 21. The German infantry was saved from being overrun by the timely intervention of divisional field guns.

The Battle for France did see attempts to create combined Panzer/infantry battle groups below regimental level, for example Vorausabteilung Eberbach of the 4.Panzer Division during the fighting for Hannut on May 12–13.[2] This was one area where the French army displayed some modest advantages in 1940, especially the combined-arms tactics of the DLM mechanized cavalry divisions. Wehrmacht tactics gradually matured, with the combined-arms Kampfgruppe eventually becoming a hallmark of German Panzer tactics.

TECHNICAL LESSONS

The Panzer divisions prevailed on the battlefield in 1940 due to better training rather than superior technology. The Wehrmacht did not place as much importance on technological advantages on the battlefield as it did on tank reliability, crew training, and effective doctrine. The quest for technological perfection often led to tanks with excellent performance on paper, but often at the expense of reliability and durability. Curiously enough, a March 1941 French army study of the 1940 battles concluded that "We will probably be surprised one day, when we know exactly the relative modesty of the German forces brought into play against us between May 10 and June 20, 1940."

In terms of mobility, the Panzers were comparable to their French counterparts. In terms of armor, the Panzers were less protected than most French tanks. The Panzers had very modest armor and most were vulnerable to typical French antitank weapons such as the 25mm antitank gun. They were also vulnerable to the better French guns such as the 47mm gun found on the Somua S 35 and Char B1 bis.

In terms of firepower, the Panzers presented a very mixed picture. The twin machine guns of the PzKpfw I were ineffective in antitank fighting, but still viable in fighting infantry. The PzKpfw II had somewhat better antiarmor performance due to its 20mm gun, but it was still poorly suited to engaging

2   For more details, see: Steven Zaloga, *Panzer III vs Somua S 35: Belgium 1940*, Osprey Duel 111, 2014.

A PzKpfw II Ausf. C of 1./ Pz.Abt.25, 7.Panzer Division in the seaside town of Saint-Valery-en-Caux on June 12, 1940, moments after driving off the coastal promenade near the casino and crashing onto the shingle beach amid a jumble of outdoor restaurant furniture. This was the town where the 51st Highland Division was trapped and forced to surrender.

the most common French tanks such as the Renault R 35 and Hotchkiss H 39 due to their thicker armor. While tank-vs.-tank fighting preoccupies most evaluations of World War II tanks, the PzKpfw I was still a capable weapon in many scenarios. German Panzer columns, consisting mainly of light tanks such as the PzKpfw I and PzKpfw II, ran amok in the race to the Channel in May 1940, often dispersing and dominating the French infantry units sent to stop them. While they were ineffective in the few large tank-vs.-tank battles such as Hannut, the mixture of German light tanks with larger German tanks enabled their battlefield survival until circumstances were more favorable for their use.

The Czech tanks proved surprisingly valuable in 1940 due to their effective armament. They did not enjoy the ergonomic advantages of the German three-man turrets, but they were still more valuable on the battlefield than the poorly armed German light tanks.

The most significant German advantage on the 1940 battlefield was the better turret layout of their tanks. The ideal configuration was the three-man Krupp turret of the PzKpw III and PzKpfw IV that gave the tank commander the freedom to lead his tank into battle without any distractions connected to aiming or loading the gun. Most other Panzers, except for the PzKpfw I, had two-man turrets. In contrast, most French tanks were crippled by their wretched one-man turrets. The French tank commander was saddled with gun aiming and loading tasks. These distractions deprived the French commander of any situational awareness of the battlefield. As French tank commanders remarked in their memoirs, once fighting started, they largely lost control of their units. They were too busy operating their own tanks. Consequently, French tank sections and squadrons could not fight as coordinated teams, instead they stumbled around the battlefield.

During the advance on Quesnoy-sur-Airaines on June 5, Pz.Rgt.25 was held up when a PzKpfw IV Ausf. D, number 321, shed a track and blocked a key railroad bridge over the Somme near Hangest. The PzKpfw 38(t) in front of it was from Pz.Abt.66, evident from its plain white tactical number. Also worth noting are the white air identification markings on the tanks' engine decks.

Probably the most disappointing German tank in the Battle of France was the PzKpfw III. This tank had been intended as the basis for the future German Panzer force. Its main drawback was its mediocre armament, the 37mm gun, selected in the mid-1930s before the lessons of the Spanish Civil War. Not only did its gun offer marginal performance at best against contemporary French and British tanks, but its small caliber also limited its ability to fire high-explosive ammunition against hostile enemy antitank guns or field works. Aside from mediocre firepower, its armor was not very impressive. Development delays limited the scale of its production, and it constituted barely 10 percent of the Panzer force in 1940.

The most useful German tank of the campaign was undoubtedly the PzKpfw IV. Although this had been envisioned merely as a support tank to provide high-explosive fire support for the other Panzers, it proved to be more durable and useful than the PzKpfw III. Its short 75mm gun was not intended for tank-vs.-tank fighting, but it was more useful in most other types of combat. The armor protection on the PzKpfw IV was not adequate against even the lightest French anti-tank guns, and the PzKpfw IV showed an alarming tendency towards catastrophic ammunition and fuel fires. Nevertheless, the PzKpfw IV had considerable growth potential due to its prudent design, and it would go on to become the basic German tank through most of the war.

G

PANZER BEFEHLSWAGEN IN THE BATTLE OF FRANCE

1. Kleiner Panzerbefehlswagen, Panzer-Artillerie-Regiment.73, 1.Panzer Division

This is a PzKpfw I command vehicle being used by the headquarters company of Panzer-Artillerie-Regiment.73. This carries the standard tactical map symbol for a towed artillery unit on the left rear hull plate; it was often repeated on the upper left of the front superstructure. The Balkan Cross is accompanied by a single chrome yellow dot indicating 1.Panzer Division.

2. Pz.Bef.Wg. Ausf. E, Stab, II./Pz.Rgt.2, 1 Panzer Division, Belgium May 1940

This was the command tank of Hptm Gitterman, the commander of II.Abteilung. In keeping with the usual practice, the tactical number for staff vehicles was I for the 1st battalion and II for the 2nd battalion. The 1.Panzer Division used plain tactical numbers for Pz.Rgt.1 and an underlined number for Pz.Rgt.2, as seen here.

A PzKpfw II Ausf. C preceded by a PzKpfw III Ausf. E of Pz.Rgt.36, 4.Panzer Division near Noyelles-sur-Sambre on the edge of the Forêt de Mormal, May 20, 1940. The PzKpfw II retains the old 1930s' pattern tank identity placard above the engine muffler as well as the new pattern painted tactical number on the turret.

German tank losses in the Battle of France 1940			
	May 40	Jun 40	Total
PzKpfw I	142	40	**182**
PzKpfw II	194	46	**240**
PzKpfw III	110	25	**135**
PzKpfw IV	77	20	**97**
PzKpfw 35(t)	45	17	**62**
PzKpfw 38(t)	43	11	**54**
PzBefWg	38	31	**69**
Total	*649*	*190*	**839**

German Panzer losses in the 1940 battles were significant, amounting to 839 tanks totally lost plus hundreds more suffering significant combat damage. The total losses amounted to about a third of the total starting strength of the Panzer force. A further 1,700 German tanks underwent factory repair and rebuilding through early 1941 to deal with both combat damage and mechanical problems.

According to a post-war French army study, overall French tank losses in 1940 amounted to 1,749 tanks of 4,071 engaged. Of these, 1,669 were caused by gunfire, 45 to mines and 35 to aircraft. This amounts to about 43 percent of the deployed force compared to German losses of about 32 percent. However, the French losses were substantially amplified by large numbers of tanks that were abandoned or scuttled by their own crews. Belgian losses were 287 tanks and tank destroyers. British losses were 691 tanks including 407 light tanks, 158 cruiser tanks and 126 infantry tanks.

FURTHER READING

The various types of German tanks employed in the Battle of France have been amply documented in many specialized monographs, notably the Panzer Tracts series. In addition, there is a significant number of German divisional and regimental histories. I used many of these to prepare this book, but they are too numerous to list here. This bibliography is limited to some of the more recent and significant campaign accounts. Much of the statistical data here comes from the Heereswaffenamt files in Record Group 242 at the National Archives and Records Administration II in College Park, MD. I also consulted the surviving records of Panzergruppe Kleist, XVI.Armee Korps and XIX.Armee Korps, also in RG 242 at NARA II.

Belle, Jacques, *La défaite francaise: Un désastre évitable*, Economica, Paris: 2007

Doughty, Robert, *The Breaking Point: Sedan and the Fall of France 1940*, Archon, Hamden: 1990

Freiser, Karl-Heinz, *The Blitzkrieg Legend: The 1940 Campaign in the West*, Naval Institute, Annapolis: 2005

Jacobsen, Hans-Adolf, *Dunkirk: German Operations in France 1940*, Casemate, Havertown: 2019

Liddell-Hart, Basil H., *The Rommel Papers*, Harcourt, Brace, Jovanovich, New York: 1953

Mary, Jean-Yves, *Le Corridor des Panzers*, Heimdal, Bayeux: 2009

Pallud, Jean-Paul, *Blitzkrieg in the West: Then and Now*, After the Battle, London: 1991

Showalter, Dennis, *Hitler's Panzers: The Lightning Attacks that Revolutionized Warfare*, Penguin, New York, 2009

INDEX

Note: Page locators in bold refer to plate captions, pictures and illustrations. All matèriel is German unless otherwise stated. Tanks denoted by (t) refer to Czech tanks subsequently adapted.